T0149325

A LONG WAY FROM THE HIGHWAY

Shaqwan Tisdale

authorHOUSE®

AuthorHouse™
1663 Liberty Drive
Bloomington, IN 47403
www.authorhouse.com
Phone: 1 (800) 839-8640

Published by AuthorHouse 10/25/2016

ISBN: 978-1-5049-8441-6 (sc)
ISBN: 978-1-5049-8439-3 (hc)
ISBN: 978-1-5049-8440-9 (e)

Library of Congress Control Number: 2016903854

Print information available on the last page.

Any people depicted in stock imagery provided by Thinkstock are models, and such images are being used for illustrative purposes only. Certain stock imagery © *Thinkstock.*

This book is printed on acid-free paper.

CONTENTS

THANK YOU

To my daughter Mellady who has been the light in the valley, my mother who have been my rock, my grandmother/mom who have been my strength, thank you!

Thank you to my sisters and brothers, aunts, uncles, cousins, friends and church family. To everyone who has prayed for me, who have given me his or her ear, and shoulder or hand in some way. I thank you also.

Thank you all for loving me through the darkest most painful moments in my life. I appreciate it more than words could ever express.

A Special thank you to everyone around the world who supported me and prayed for me, thank you. Most importantly, thank you for holding me so close to your heart from the moment my own had failed.

Last but not least to my God, the great I Am, My Daddy. I love you with my life. I pray that you get the glory out of my life. I know if it had not been for you, I would not have made it thus far. Thank you for loving me. Thank you for trusting me and keeping me through the toughest struggle I have ever imagine experiencing.

Life, what is it really? How well do you really know it? Could life be a friend to anyone from the very beginning? Is there really a difference between its good and bad? What can you really tell me about this life? I do not think there is anyone who actually knows; however, no one seems to care or acts as if life is so harmless and that we should not be afraid or fear it. I say that maybe we should. Maybe we should try to find a way to beat it, but no, I know that would never work. Just maybe we should reason with it or better yet try to find out what exactly does it want. One thing that I know for sure is that we certainly cannot hide from it. Whatever we do, we certainly do not need to stand in its way.

I would like to think that I met this life once. Everything about it seems to be familiar. It's anonymous color, its unrecognizable shape, its enormous amounts of fragrances, its impeccable undiscovered language and especially its unique cleverness. Oh yea, now that I really think about it, I am convinced that I have. I was very young and unware of its beauty yet ugly intentions. The minute life and I met something told me that I would from then on view things in a completely new way and that, I did; however, it taught me something that no one or anything could have ever taught me, I was only as strong as my heart. See I have come to understand that life has its own agenda. It is always on a constant move; in fact, it never stops working. I did not know then but I know now that life's main assignment is to go after your heart and if it can affect your heart then it can affect your strength and not just your physical strength but also the strength of your mind. It is amazing how life is actually not your friend or your enemy at all. What life is can be entirely up to you. I know it may sound crazy but I understand now that its intentions are neither good nor bad. Life is more consistent at what it does than you and I will ever be. Although life is what it is, we make it responsible for every outcome.

For me yes, because there was no one else to blame, so I did consider life as my enemy. I made it responsible for everything not good that happened to me; therefore, in my mind life had hurt me to the core. I felt as though I had gone through hell even as a little kid and the moment that I thought I had finally overcame and conquered my pain and fears, life came again and took everything that had made me who I was. With every ounce of pain that rest within me, literally drove me to the point that made me want to give up but the strength of my heart never lost its strength in God. I have a daughter who looks up to me and who watches my every move. It is hard sometimes because I do not have all of the instructions and I do not want to fail but I tell you this, I know now that all I have since the day I entered into this world is love. Therefore, in spite of the hell that has surrounded and invaded my world, it did not destroy my ability to love. I have come to realize that everyone has a story. It is a story that makes us who we are and our heart often protects it. My heart protects my love; therefore, it is my greatest story. So I pray that as my heart is given the opportunity and the ability to speak that you do not sit in judgment and not only strengthen your heart, but also live in such a way that your living empowers someone else to Trust God in the full capacity of their heart.

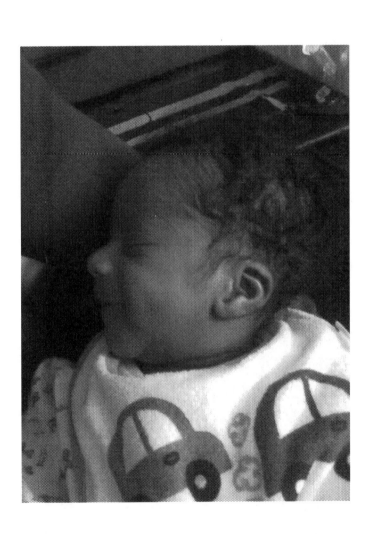

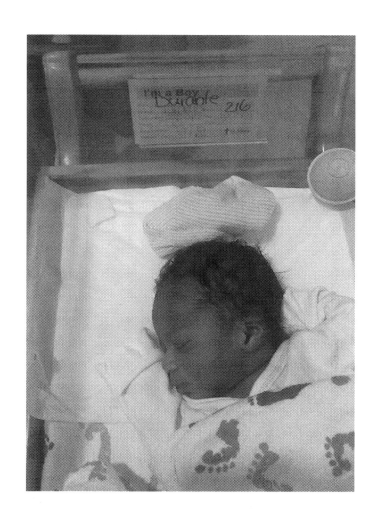

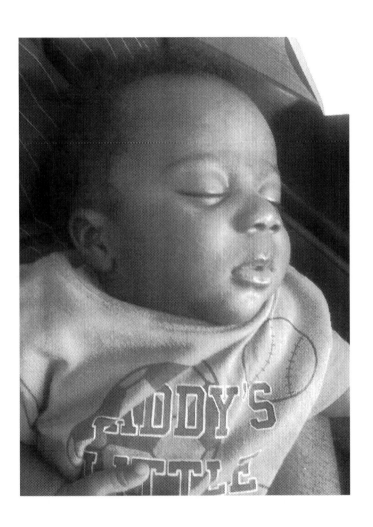

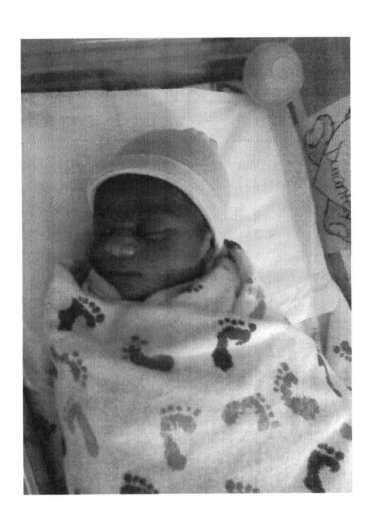

CHAPTER 1

Unconscious

Four months later and I felt like I had just awakened from a coma. It seemed as though I had just opened the eyes of someone else other than myself. I could barely move any part of my body and even thinking about moving them, felt as if they were never a purpose for them to move at all. This place did not look familiar, nor was the aroma that filled my nostrils. Why was it so quiet? Why were the colors so dark and dull? Nothing was clear and in my head, the only sound that I did hear was the sound of a radio channel that had lost its signal. I did not feel normal at all in fact; I felt so empty and heartless and I had no explanation as to why. These walls were so close and seemed to have already known me. This room itself seemed to have welcomed me in and knew more about me than I had known of myself. Why did I feel so threatened and intimidated? Immediately I noticed the tired ceiling staring at me as if it had been working overtime. There was no evidence that confirmed my imprisonment but I could feel all of the restraints against me. I could feel the tears sliding down my face and I could feel the knots in my belly and a pain in my chest that seemed to be deeper than the ocean, but still there were no answers. I wanted to scream but I had no energy to force anything out of me. It was so cold that my body felt like ice." God where are you" I thought to myself as it echoed throughout the room. I remembered Him once again and I needed Him.

I remember reading that he would never leave me nor forsake me (yea that's always the one) and that He would be with me even to the end of the world. I was not sure if it was the end or not but I was looking for Him yet again. I was looking for Him to show up. However, nothing, nothing happened and certainly, no one came. That feeling, Yes I do remember. There was a sudden knock and following the knock, I heard a small voice. The voice called out to me and said "Dad, are you ok," It was not until the second knock did I realize it was a little girls voice and a beat hit my chest like a baseball bat. My heart begun to beat so fast and so loud that I remembered the moment it stopped. I remember lying in a hospital bed with so many people around me that I could barely see their faces or even remember what they looked like; however, I remember the doctor coming in the room and telling me something that seemed like the worst dream that I could have possibly dreamed. As the doctor stood in front of me, I heard him say, "Your wife and two sons did not make it". At that moment, I remember my heart gave up and the tears flowed like the Niagara Falls. I felt my body drop and before I knew it, I was falling. I was falling and screaming all at the same time. There was no destination just an endless fall. How can I describe that very moment? I never imagine the day that I would hear such poisonous words. It felt like instead of blood there was a liquid form of pain just flowing through my veins." Oh God catch me, and make it go away" I kept screaming as I was falling. My world was shattered. My life was no longer alive and my breath took off with the wind. Those words had gutted me up until my very insides where leaking out. "Somebody help me; help me because I can't take it". It was so much pain that it was the only way I knew I was still alive. Once again I was left with the questions in my head as to rather or not God was real. How could God be real and take almost everything that matter the most to me. I thought that He cared and loved me. I depended on him to take care of my family and me and to always protect us. I have held on to him all my life even as a little boy. Although I went through a life of hell, somehow in spite of it all I managed to still love Him and trust Him. Now I was at a point that I felt it was all for nothing. I could have done so much that I did not do because I wanted to please God. I wanted to make it to heaven. It felt good and seem like doing right made me happy but what happens when you get here and happiness no longer exist because the people that made you happy had been snatched away. Still I was falling, and as I was falling, I remember not wanting to stop. I wanted to fall until everything was gone. I wanted the people, the doctor, the pain, and the tears to all go away especially the words that had pushed me right off the edge. There was nothing beyond this point. There was no vision, no dream, no ambition, and no drive for nothing, just my unwanted existence. Thinking intensified the pain and so did knowing. I could feel that they were watching me fall and they may have been trying to catch me but there was no use. There was no use for them trying to caress my body, rub my head or massage my shoulders. There was no use for them hugging me, kissing me, massaging my feet, or telling me everything was going to be all right. There was just no use for them crying with me and telling me that they understood because none of it mattered. Nothing was going to bring my family back; therefore, I was never coming back. I was never going to stop falling. I was hoping that the fall would eventually end it all. If I knew then what I know now I do not think I would have ever gotten married and had a family. I would not want any one not even my enemies to feel the pain and agony that I was feeling. I wanted so badly for someone to say 'it is a miracle, their alive". I waited as I continued to scream hoping that someone would say it. I was hoping that God would hear or feel my pain and say "ok it's enough I know you can't bear it anymore" and just make something happen. No matter how hurt or upset I was, I was hoping that God really would prove himself to me. I thought about faith and what the Bible said about it and I tried to use it even in the condition that I was in but I never did hear what I was hoping to hear. Eventually their faces started to appear before me and I would cry and scream even more. You always see or hear in movies or on the news of such tragedies but never did I think in a million years that it would be my life, my tragedy. We had so much planned, so much we wanted to do. (Deep breath) I just remember, as I was still yet falling and still yet bleeding pain, wanting to hold my wife and children so tight in my arms so bad. I wanted to touch their face and hands. I wanted to see their smiles and feel their breath against my cheeks. I wanted to hear them speak, yell, and laugh. I wanted to hear the arguments and disagreements. I wanted to hear the crying and wining. I needed to hear it all. I wanted to come home from work and have them run to me in my arms. I wanted to sit at the dinner table and have long conversations about work, school, and everything that had happen throughout everyone's day. I wanted to feed the baby and rock him to sleep. I wanted to sing a song, say a prayer, and tuck my kids into their beds. I wanted to hold my wife, kiss her neck, and tell her how much I loved and missed her all day. I wanted to live my life again. I wanted another chance. I wanted to go back and correct any mistakes that I may have made as a husband or a father. I wanted to go back and love harder than I have ever loved before. I believe that if I was given the chance, I would never get mad or angry for anything but from the very moment my wife and I met each other I would have cherished it and held on to everything as if I could lose it all at any second. I tried to think about anything that could possibly make me feel better but what in the world could I or anyone else say or do that could make me feel at all. It was so unfair, everything was just not right. How was this at all the will of God or better yet who in the world did God think I was to be able to take on such pain? Why give me this life only to take it away? Cannot say I did not think all of this because I did. I thought about how I used to be so afraid to die and at a point again in my life I felt like I was close to it; although, I actually was. How do I block this all out, how do I make it all go away? I wasn't so sure if my eyes opening was such a good idea or that It was for a good purpose; however, with my eyes close I saw nothing, nothing but darkness, images without color that were made up of nothing but for some reason these images kept appearing and disappearing.

They would slowly fade in and out and still I could not make anything of them. In reality, I did not know if I was breathing or even alive for that matter. I remember one day the family and I were on our way inside of this really tall building that my sister lived in. The elevators were about to close so while holding the baby in the carrier I ran and tried to stop it but some woman in the elevator stopped it for me and we waited until my family got on. I remember standing in the elevator feeling so uncomfortable because this woman just kept staring at us all. Finally, before getting to her stop, the woman looked at my wife and said "you are so pretty, you look just like a model" of course my wife smiled and said "thank you" as she looked back at me the woman replied again by saying "you all are just one beautiful family." I didn't quite get it until now that my family was perfect, too perfect if you ask me, but not perfect in a sense that we were flawless and on this enormous pedal stool but perfect in a since that we were the ideal family that people only dreamed about because we were so young and happy with beautiful well-mannered kids and not to mention my wife and I was so madly in love, on the good days anyway (smiling) but that to me and the rest of the world was such a beautiful light to see, but just remembering that, hurts like an excruciating tooth ache. I was so far back in my mind that I probably wouldn't have come back but suddenly I heard that voice again, "Dad are you ok"? I was still unable to speak but it did not matter because the voice was coming near. I heard the door open and I could hear footsteps that sounded as if they were trying to be as cautious as possible. For some reason I was getting colder by the second and I could feel my body trembling but I could see I was not moving at all. When the voice had found its way to the side of me, I instantly recognized it and I jumped up so quickly leaving my body there lying on the bed. Grabbing my hand and squeezing it tight I could feel that it was not just any type of grip but it was a grip that said I love you more than anything. It was a grip that said your all that I have and I do not want to lose you but the tighter the grip got, I could also feel that it saying, "I'm hurting and I'm scared and I don't know what to do". It was so obvious that I could relate to the grip and because I could, the voice was not needed because voice I once heard had now become silent but I could feel the tears running down my neck as the voice had formed a body and its arms and hands were wrapped around my shoulders. There was no sound at least not with lips but there was in fact multiple sounds that could only be heard by your heart and the only words that were spoken was from the mouth of running tears that seemed to speak with intensifying yet soft words. I cannot even explain what was happening or if anything was happening at all but what I can say, is that this pain I could tell wasn't going anywhere anytime soon but it was in fact positioned and ready to stay awhile. It was definitely a long conversation because it felt like I had been baptized all over again. Finally, the hands released me and lift up its head and there I saw eyes that looked into my soul and with those eyes I knew that they could see every ounce of the pain that resided in me because for a brief moment they were closed as if it was too unbearable to see. I tried so hard not to cry anymore, not to show that I was weak but that I was the same person who was tough and strong and who could carry the world on each of my shoulders. Of course, it was impossible to do in fact there was not much I could do at all. This was not what I ever imagined or even thought that I could ever feel. Just like a place of not knowing, I felt lost. All I could think about was how soon this would all be over. When will these painful feelings go away? I did not want these emotions, I needed to gain control of what was happening but I did not have that ability. After a while she looked at me and said "daddy, I want mommy, jay, and musik"! At that very moment, it felt like the room was spinning and as if someone was choking me. I could not say a word and even if I could, I did not know what to say. Those exact words felt like a weapon too strong and powerful to stand against. My heart surrendered and immediately gave up its rights.

CHAPTER 2

Living the Pain

All this time my daughter and I had been living with my aunt and her children and I barely remember any of it until the day my daughter walked into the room. It's like my world had disappeared and when it finally appeared It was a different world I had never seen before. One morning I looked into the mirror for the first time and I saw a person I didn't even know but right before me was flashing images that I couldn't seem to stop from appearing. It felt like an inappropriate movie that I shouldn't have been seeing but the clips had caused me to remember why. I was walking with a cane and my right knee felt like the bones were raddling around inside. Why could I not feel on the left side of my face or from the front to the back of my head? Why was I barely seeing out of my left eye? Why were my lungs and ribs crushed and bruised? Why was it so difficult for me to move my neck and why were there deep scars all over my body? I felt like a complete stranger to myself. I was always told how nice I looked and I used to actually believe it at one point but judging from the mirror I was ashamed. I couldn't stand to look at the person barely looking back at me and if truth be told I was terrified of it. I remember breaking down in the bathroom and just thinking to myself could what I see and feel be real. "Qwan"! "Qwan"! Suddenly I heard my name called. For a second I wasn't sure if it was just me or if I was really being called so I opened the door and it wasn't until I heard the call again did I realized it was my aunt who had call my name. She asked me to come down stairs because I had a visitor. I tried wiping my tears and washing my face but I could barely touch it. My face from what I could see look as though it was an old beat up inflated basketball. I didn't want anyone to see me but I didn't have much of a choice. When I finally got to the bottom of the last stair, I could see three gentleman dressed in fancy elegant suites with briefcases. I had no idea why they were there or why wanted to see me. I had never seen any of them before at least I didn't think I had. I sat on the couch that was the furthest from them with my head down. It was silent for a while and then one of the gentleman finally spoke up, "were sorry to bother u Mr. Tisdale and we're so sorry for your loss" but I didn't respond back. "We're lawyers from Johnnie Cochran firm and we want to take your case. We know this may be a difficult time for you but we assure you we will make it as easy as possible for you and your daughter to live and try to move forward in life by making sure u both are financially taking care of. Does that sound ok to you?" He asked and then paused to give me an opportunity to respond. I was very still and continued to say nothing; I did not lift up my head. Suddenly there was a knock at the door. "Are you ok hunny" my aunt asked me as she got up and headed down stairs to open the door. I gave no reply. I could hear my aunt telling someone down stairs who the guys where upstairs and why. I could hear her informing them of my response to the idea of them being there. Finally, they were coming up the stairs. "This is my sister, Qwan's mother" my aunt said to the lawyers as they were shaking her hand I lifted up my head. My mom had come to see me as she did every day. My daughter told me she always came and sit with me for hours and hours at a time. She said sometimes she find us both down stairs crying and not saying anything at all. I was relieved that she was there I knew she would talk for me and I wouldn't have to say a word. My mom walked over to me and sat down next to me and hugged my neck then she held my hand and rubbed her fingers through my hair. The lawyer reiterates what he had said to me so my mom knew what was going on. Maybe I wasn't really listening the first time he was talking because this time I heard him say that two of them was from the firm in NY and one of them just flew in from somewhere far I can't remember where but I just knew I was ready for them to leave. Finally, one of the other gentlemen spoke. "We're just waiting on Mr. Tisdale to respond, accept our services and sign the paperwork. We really need to get started right away if we're going to get things moving for him". My mom then grabbed my face by both her hands and lifted up my head. She looked into my eyes and said "you don't have to make a decision now or make one at all if you don't want to, but whatever you decide I'm going to stand beside you and we're going to pray about it and trust God" I whispered to her and said "I don't want no money, I don't any of it, none of it will bring my family back" but she looked at me and smiled. I knew that look, it was a look as if she wanted to say I reminded her of my grandmother but she told me she understood how I felt and as she told me before It was something I had to do in order to make sure that my daughter was going to be tokened care of. I immediately thought about my lawyers that I already had and how I felt the seriousness in their hearts. I could feel that they sympathized with me. Before I could say a word the lawyer that sat in the middle started to speak. "Did you tell him to pray? Because I think that is a good idea. You definitely want to make sure that God is in any decision that you make" my mom smiled and raised her eyebrows at me as if she was asking me what I wanted to do. In a very low voice I said "yes we can pray" the lawyer asked us all to joined hands and then he begun to pray. After he was done praying I told my mom I would sign. They lawyers pulled all the necessary documents out that I needed and I signed my name on each line. "Do u feel good about your decision? I think you made a great decision" my aunt said passing the papers back to the lawyers. The lawyers began to tell me about how much money that my case was worth, all the people that they were going after and how my daughter and I would be ok for the rest of our life. I didn't realize it until they were shaking my mom and aunt's hands that I made the wrong decision. I realized that they knew that I was a very spiritual person after the conversation my mom was having with me and they used it against me. After they left my mom looked at me and could tell that something was wrong. She waited until my aunt walked up the other set of stairs into the kitchen and she asked me what was wrong. I told her what I thought and how I felt and she said that we would call my other lawyers and straighten it out. Later on that night I found myself in the living room listening to the CDs on the little stereo my daughter said the church had bought me. One of the CDs that would seem to help me was the Tasha Cobb cd. I remember I would play it over and over again and cry myself to sleep. I would go to sleep with my family in my mind and heavy on my heart. I would dream that I would go back to our house and they would all be sitting at the dinner table waiting for me to come home as if I was at work. It would seem like the happiest dream ever but the weirdest because I would be standing in the door way crying and each time I would run to them and hugged all of them so tight. It was always a dream I never wanted to awake from but it seemed as though my aunt, one of my cousins, or my daughter would always wake me up to make sure I was ok and wanted to know why I wasn't in the bed. I tell you she was like my shadow. Wherever I was she wasn't far from me and she could tell when I would move or wasn't near. It reminded me so much of my oldest son. (Smiling) She was always making sure I was ok. At that time, it was so many people almost every day calling, coming to the house and sending me letters. Many people I didn't know or didn't remember that I knew them but it was nice to know that people cared and thought about my daughter and I. There were some days I felt like I was living but dead at the same time because every day was the same as the day before except for the days that my daughter had I had doctor's, therapy, or counselor appointments. My life felt meaningless and without purpose. The trees became a part of my world and every color I could stare at and get lost in rather it was a wall, floor, door, or ceiling, it became my best friend. There were so many times I wanted to pick up a pen and paper and write but I felt no words would matter or make a difference in anything. I often heard my voice in my head and songs and my heart but I could never force my mouth open or tongue to even move to make a sound. After a while I realize I hadn't prayed or read my bible in such long time I really felt empty. I just remember every time I would cry and the pain would seem so unbearable. I would find a way to whisper Jesus name rather it was in my heart, my mind, or with my lips that I could barely move half of the time. I needed to be back in church I needed to feel something more besides pain. I remember the first time I did go back to church I could literally hear my thoughts echoing in my head as I waited in the elevator. As soon as I opened the door my head began to spin and my body started to tremble. I remembered how I looked and wanted to go back but my aunt wouldn't let me go. She opened the door and my daughter and I walked into the sanctuary. I could tell everyone was so surprised to see us and happy. I on the other hand didn't want to be noticed but after being gone for about five months I know that was Ludacris. I remember we sat in the back far away from the seats my family and I would usually sit. I tried my hardest to keep it together. I tried to not cry but the tears just wouldn't stop falling. I wasn't sure if anyone noticed but I tried so hard to wipe them away the minute I felt them running down my cheeks. Before I knew it my Pastor had called my name. He began to speak into my life and the more he spoke the faster my heart would beat. Then he called me up to the front. A couple of guys helped me get up and walk to the front. When I got there I felt my body shaking again. I could feel every one behind me staring at me. My Pastor held me in his arms and looked at me. I remember him saying "son would you sing the song that you sung for the new years' service? Another day that the Lord has kept me, I know it would really bless the people this morning and most importantly it would help you too". I didn't know if I could do it. I didn't know if the sound was still there. I only heard my voice in my head and it had been so long since I sung anything. I got so hot I thought I was going to pass out. I looked up at my Pastor and said "yes sir, okay". He handed the mic to me and I gripped my fingers around it with one hand while the other held the cane I was walking with. It was something about touching that mic that made me think about one particular song from my cd Lord help me to stand. I needed God's help at that moment I didn't know what to do but deep down inside I wanted him to save me. I wanted to stand In spite of everything that I was feeling. I took a deep breath and began to sing. The room got cold and but warm at the same time I could fill a breeze across my face and the more I sung it, caused the not in the bottom of my stomach to unravel and I could fill the sound bursting its way out between every beat of my heart. I felt as if it was just me all by myself signing in the clouds as I was floating up higher and higher in the sky. When I was done I turned around with tears dripping down my face and soaking up my shirt. I began to walk back to my seat and as I looked up almost every person in my eye site was crying. As a matter of fact, it was a brief moment where all you heard were people crying. I remember sitting down in my seat and feeling so empty. It was real. I had lost it all. I was once asleep in my pain but I was now awake and living within it.

CHAPTER 3

Broken Promise

So weak and tired sometimes I would sit and have conversations in the room with just my wife and me. I would scream and call out her name but of course, there was never an answer. I remember saying to her "I wish that you was here, I often ask myself what can I do to bring u back. I would give anything just to feel your heart beat again. This is not how we planned our life to be. You said u would never leave me. You promised me no matter what, that you would stay rite here. This is the worst feeling ever and I would never do this to you. Why am I stuck where I am? I'm so sorry that I didn't understand u the way I should have. Now that you are gone, I feel exactly what u felt and it's a lonely place. This place I never wanted to be. It's amazing how everyone around you can see you but not really see you, not know your hurting, or not know that life is so hard without the person that meant so much to you. Do you know because I do not know what I am supposed to do to pass by the time, or what am I supposed to do while I am still here? You did not leave me with any instructions, a manual, or anything. Like what do I do? Our daughter needs her mother. What do I tell her? What do I teach her? How can I teach her anything? This is not fair this is so hard. I do not know where to start nor do I know where to begin. You said that I was the perfect father but that is only because I had you. You bought the best out of me you made me be the king that I was. I know, that I will never be loved the way you loved me and I know that I will never feel the way u made me feel or maybe I just don't want to. I remember how you always said that you admire my strength and the strong will power that I had but where that strength is and will power now, I do not know. I do not know who I am anymore. I had wrapped myself into you and all I know is you. I am not going to make it out here. We always said that we would be ok as long as we had each other. Therefore, by now you should know, I am falling apart. Why am I supposed to be the person that has to be so strong? Can I just let go? I do not even know if I am going to wake up the next day. I know people who have died from a heartbreak. Maybe that would be me and I will be with u. It feels like I am holding my heart in my hands but that is just it. My hands are the wrong hands. Why do I have it and not you? I cannot stand to hear my own heart beat when yours I can no longer hear. How can this make sense? How can I wake up every morning and face the day without knowing at some point I will hold you and kiss you. We work so hard to achieve so much. Why did we go through literally hell only to be separated so soon? Where is our happy ending? I had many prayers and I just knew you were the best of them all. Actually u was. You said I saved you but you actually saved me. I never got a chance to tell you how. You fell in love with a boy and groomed me into a man. You loved me in every way possible. I often think about if I did not have your love where and what would I have become. You chose to love me In spite of any hang-ups I may have had. I never knew I could be perfect and not perfect in the since that I could do no wrong but perfect in a since that I was everything you wanted and needed. I tried so hard to stop you but you carried my problems with you and not only did you carry them but you tried to help solve them. Even when I tried to prevent you from doing that, you still found a way to do just what you needed to do. I never had to tell you that I needed you, but always knew. I never had to ask you to hold my hand or kiss me. You knew just when to comfort me when I felt sad depressed or frustrated. You knew what to do when I didn't feel confident or more so afraid or nervous. You always gave me a push like no other. I'm screaming rite now because I'm hurting so bad. It's crazy how people are looking at me to be this person that's incredible but what's incredible about having a life full of pain. I don't want any trophies I don't need any medals give it to someone that actually did something extravagant. All I want is my family back. Life would be so much better. So much for this journey that we had created for each other. I'm the only one who is walking on the path and that's not the way it works. I think about how people would often see us out and about and admire the way we were always together and coordinated everything. People were amazed at our life and we were just being us. We were just trying to be the family that we had always dreamed of having. We were so close and we loved each other until the point where if one was sick we all got sick. I miss the laughter I miss the moments where I could come home and feel like I was entering a place where I was wanted. I remember the nights we would have family night and we would sit down stairs in one room and watch funny movies and laugh until we were crying. I miss it so much and I try every day to hold on to the memories. Most of the times they hold me together and they keep me alive. I don't want to forget them. I don't want to forget you or our children. I want to hold you all in my arms until my heart feels better. I want love, your love; it has always been faithful and true to me. I never had to second guess how you felt about me. I always knew that that your love would go as far as it could for me. I admire most how your love always fought for me and I never had to ask if you were going to go all the way with me because everywhere I went and everywhere I turned you was always there. It's funny how I used to get upset when you wanted to be everywhere that I was and how I didn't go many places because you wanted me home or to be right there with me. If I had known what I know now then there is no way I would have ever even thought about getting upset or even being bothered that u just always wanted to be around me or with me. Although sometimes I may have acted like a jerk because my boys were around, you made me seem like the king, of course when they left you got with me but even still I appreciated the way that you cared for me. Things are so different now. I am at the point where I feel like I'm going crazy and my mind seem to be everywhere except for where it belongs. I'm so tired and I feel like I don't know what to do. I don't know where my energy is or where was that push that I always had. I was always ready and alert but now I just feel so drained. What's happening to me? Something is broken and it's not just my heart. I hate to get out the bed or even walk outside. It could be a day where the sun is shining so bright and its hot but with a cool breeze, beautiful flowers blossoming everywhere and the sky so happy with its soft yet loud clouds and a very large background of blue surrounding everything that's near and far. Butterflies and birds could be flying in the air so peacefully and the creatures on the ground could be traveling about with no worries, along with everything else that complimented each other that just made the weather so perfect but for me it would feel like a snow storm but with the rain and hail coming down at the same time. It would seem as though the ground was covered with dirty snow up to my knees and the clouds had disappeared leaving behind the darkest colors that surrounded every area near or far. It would feel so cold and windy with no sign of happiness not even from a creature crawling, flying, or even walking. I couldn't seem to find peace except for when I was alone thinking or dreaming. That's how it is even now I just have these random thoughts and for some reason it does bring a sense of peace but always seem to fight so hard to escape. I was never supposed to be here in this place of misery. My spirit is broken and so is the promise that you've made to me. It was just like going to sleep at night knowing that the sky was black and waking up in the morning to a blue sky. There was no sign or clue, you just left and the worst part about it is you never said good bye.

CHAPTER 4

Perfect Love

Tired, weak, and trying to breath on my own. My heart is beating but at this point, it was better off quiet. How did I get here, how did I get to this place of just being empty? I thought I was getting better, I thought I had gotten stronger, and look at me now. I am so broken, I am so lonely, and I am so hurt. It took a while but I realize I have made the biggest mistake of my life. I became venerable. I became blind to anything that was coming my way. I could not see it, I could not smell it, and I could not feel it, but I was lacking love.

What love that has never failed me,

What love that has stood beside me

Never changed on me

But shield and covered me

What love undeserving but yet held me

What love that has no boundaries

And is willing to fight for me

What love that continuously grows

And never gets old

What love you can trust

And is always true

What love is real

And you can always feel

It's that love that carry us through our toughest and roughest times

It's that love that pushes us through the river made by our tears but

yet we often fear

It's that love that never runs out, but is everlasting

always covering

It's that love that has strength when we are at our weakest

And is felt the deepest.

It's that love that teaches us how to survive in rain and build

through pain

No other love but God's love.

That love u don't have to go out and find nor do u have to fight for

it to keep it. That love cost u nothing and is always available. That

love just made me stronger and wiser.

CHAPTER 5

Ending Point

I pretended as long as I could but it got to the point where I could no longer pretend. You was not coming back and nor was our kids. Mellady had made it a little easier but after she started school, she was gone most of the day so it was just me, me and my thoughts and visions of our family. I did not care anymore I just wanted you there. I am nothing without you. I felt so lost and I needed you in my life more than ever. Nobody really knew how I felt. They did not even know how sometimes I wanted to ended all but I knew our daughter needed me and I actually needed her too. If it was not for her I just did not know at times, what I was capable of doing, but that was never me. You probably don't hear me, more less hear my thoughts. I wondered if you knew how much I have missed you. I have missed being able to talk to you about everything and there is so much even now that I have to say. Somethings that I have not even told you because I never wanted you to worry but I wanted you to know that I was always going to love you. I just hated that everything that reminded me of you and that you wore, touched, or had been back at home. I was so scared to go back though and I was afraid that you might have been upset that I did not go back. I remember one day my aunt received a call from the property owner asking what I was going to do because all of our stuff was still in the house and I had a balance to pay for the rent. I have not been to the house since the day we had left for the concert. My mom and step dad along with my god brother would often go and check to make sure everything was ok. I just knew I could not stand to be in the last place that we were in before the accident. I kept telling myself I was going to go back. Actually I was told not to go back, for a while that is anyway. Since the accident news, reporters where always hanging around but my waiting time had finally run out. After the property owners called, I had no choice but to go get everything out. I remember pulling up to the house and right before my eyes I could see at least twenty images of our family coming in and out of the house. I wish I could have gotten each of those moments back if nothing but for a little while. I finally got out the truck and my mom opened the door. From the moment I walked in I wanted to break down. It was our home. I was lost for words. "Are you going to be ok," my step dad, asked me but I did not know. I did not know if I wanted to stay or leave right away. For a minute, I stood standing in one spot looking around. My god brother walked me up the stairs and I started to get weak the minute I walked in and out of the kid's room. Lastly, I opened the door to our bed room and I felt a knife stab me in the heart. I held my chest and there they came just as I knew they would tears that had refused to stop flowing. I could no longer stay there. My mom ran up the stairs and took me by the hands. "We can leave now she said and took me out side and put me in the car. They all stayed in for a while but by the time they eventually came out, I had already cried myself to sleep. I did not go back until a week later but this time when I did go back it was something different about the house. As I began to take a closer look at things, I saw that there were things missing.

"Where is our TV"? I screamed to the top of my lungs. Everyone immediately looked at me and said they did not know. I got up the stairs as fast as I could with the Cain still in my hand. I looked inside of our daughter's room and everything was fine. Our son's door was opened and before I walked in, I could see from the door that his Xbox 360 was missing. As I got even closer inside the room, I realized his guitar was gone as well. I kept screaming "no"! Everyone was trying to calm me down but I did not want to. I found my way into our room and sure enough, CDs, books, shoes, clothes, and baby stuff was missing. I also noticed that the brand new keyboard and guitar my wife had brought me was gone not to mention all of her expensive jewelry. All the DVDs and DVD players, cameras and computer stuff was gone. It had become too much and before I knew it right there on the floor I broke down and fell to the floor. I looked up to the ceiling and screamed so loud "Why"! Why was the same question I had asked a million times because I just could not seem to understand? Before I knew it, my mind had drifted off and all I could think about was how life was before it was drastically changed. Everything was perfect, and when I say perfect, I mean just that. I was finally living a life that I had worked so hard at for so long. I was a young man who was married to the most beautiful woman in the world, with three most precious and loving kids a father could ever asked for, a good paying office job for my age, and the start of an amazing career as an author and gospel artist. What did I do wrong, where did I go wrong? Was I paying for past sins that I had committed? Did I even deserve this? Life was simply not being fair to me. I felt as if it had swallowed me whole and threw me back up. There were no words that could possibly express how I truly felt. My heart was so weak to the point that it would shut down at any time. Even then, the memories are what had hurt the most. It was so easy to close my eyes and see life because life is what I once had. It was all that I knew and certainly it was what I longed to have again. Sometimes there was no warning, it just happened and before I knew it, my eyes would shut again. All I would hear is laughter and crying all at the same time. Sometimes it's even conversations or running and playing and yelling, all joyful sounds trapped inside of my ear but it's when I open my eyes that I see my world is simply a nightmare that I can never escape. August second two thousand and thirteen would have been one of the best days of my life but instead it became the most painful and terrifying day that I would never forget for as long as I live. Although that year ended in a disaster, it was certainly not how it begun. I remember on March the twenty third we were riding in the truck coming over the Burlington Bristol bridge when all of a sudden my wife started having strange pains in in her belly. She was already two weeks away from her due date, so the thought came across my mind that something was wrong. "I'm taking you to the hospital," I said to her as she was rubbing her stomach up and down. If truth were told, I was scared especially after having four miscarriages prior to this pregnancy. Trying not to breathe so hard she responded, "You have things to do; besides we have the kids with us". Even though I was scared, I looked at her and smiled because even at that moment she was being so strong. I remember pulling over into the Wawa parking lot. I grabbed her hand as her breathing started to get heavier. Without looking at me, she said "Do you think I'm going to have the baby today, your sister said I was" I could see that in spite of how strong she was she was nervous and scared at the same time. I picked up my cell phone and called my aunt who did not live to far from where we were. She said she was out and was not too far away and she would pick up the kids. "I'm sorry baby I know you had so much you wanted to get done today," my wife said as soon as I hung up the phone. 'You and our baby is more important than anything I would have to do on any day" I replied kissing her hand. Not long after, my aunt arrived at the Wawa and took the kids. Even she was excited and told us to keep her posted. As I tried not to rush and scare my wife even more I drove as careful as I possibly could. I guess it did not hit me yet that we could have been having the baby because I was so stuck on the due date especially because it was four days before my birthday. Sure enough when we got to St. Mary's hospital, my wife said to me that she had been having small contractions but they were starting to get worse. I could not believe she did not tell me from the beginning but then again I knew that she knew me, so it probably was a good idea that she didn't. She asked me to call my mom right away because she wanted her there. Immediately my mom picked up the phone and after I told her what was going on, she said she was on her way. At the time, I did not think about it but now I look back and smile because it was as if they were best friends and she would always drop whatever she was doing to be there for her. Even when things would happen and I know it was not my fault to them it was. I remember I would get so upset and mad but after a while, I understood that because she did not have any family around that it was something that she needed. "Qwan!, you got to get up baby" I could hear my mom saying as my mind found its way back to reality. When I realize where I was again I became so angry and then sad. I just could not believe someone would hurt me so bad. None of this would have happened if my family were still alive. I cried so badly until snot was draining out of my nose and mucus was running out of my mouth. Someone had taken the things that were left of my family. I knew I had to get out on my own again and take care of my daughter by myself and I definitely had to get the rest of my stuff out of that house before someone came back and took it all. I had realized that life continued to go on and I had to do the same because if I did not, I was afraid I could lose my daughter next.

CHAPTER 6

Inside the Box

That night I could hear the knocking in my head, and every time I rushed to open the door, there was no one there. Sometimes I stand there and wait, just to see if someone would show and each time is the same, sort of how life was for you and now me. It was as if something had you trapped inside of an empty dark room. Wow, I could not see it before but I see it now. I imagined it to be like a box, a box that has been sealed shut at every corner. This explains the reason why you said you could not breathe. You said you were going to die there and I get it. You did not know how to fight, you did not know how to scream and in reality no would have heard you anyway because when the box had found its way opened no one noticed, no one heard you crying and no one cared to know why there was a distance and such a big change. You felt as though the same box that kept you trapped inside was the only thing that kept you safe because the box had already known of your darkest secret or should I say, your most painful moment. (Tears) You found yourself back inside the box and it is there where you laid yourself to rest but it was only for a short time because months later the pain looked you in the face. You realize this scar was permeant the minute you were threatened to never speak of the box and the one who actually created it. That box had striped you of your faith, your, love, your life, and most importantly your voice. There is a saying that drugs and alcohol brings out the worst in a person but many do not realize that it is the same for this thing called pain. That thing alone could create a monster and although you felt like a monster, you tried your hardest not to become one but it seems as if being one kept everyone away. I often told you I wish I were there, I wish I could go back and never have left and stayed right by your side, I would have protected you being as though no one else did. My mind often goes back to when you were a little girl and how sweet you were, how innocent and spiritual we both were. (Laughing) It was like a match mad from heaven. I had never seen a little girl like you before so gentle and soft with your words and actions which is what drew me so close to you. I mean you love God like you loved your fruit and you know you loved your fruit. You were so strong and faithful to God. It just made you so much more beautiful. I guess that is why everyone admired you so much, even family members, especially the one that was sick in the head. I did not know a year later I would experience your pain then years later we would help each other through it. You know I think about the person who created your box all the time. I think about how afraid and fearful you were and even how after nine years they were still able to keep you trapped inside. There were so many times you tried to be comfortable inside the box and embrace what was done to you especially after you finally said something about it but for some reason it was not something that could easily be done. I think about how we always prayed against the spirit of hate, it always seemed to find us so attractive because of our in boxed pain but God always provided our way of escape. It was not until the day I opened my eyes and I saw, I saw the person who had created your box staring me right in the face. Your brother was there, your mom, and one of your cousins, that's all that I can remember, but at first I thought they came to embrace Mellady and I but the only person crying was your mom and I could hear the hurt in her cry. She kept saying she was sorry and I couldn't understand why or what exactly she was referring to but I had soon found out when the creator of your box said to me that he took our son's body and wanted to tell me personally but in reality I know he wanted to see me die. Somehow, he was able to create a fake birth certificate and signed his name and they let him take our son. My mom was screaming and crying so much that I just remember after they left feeling cold and everyone that was inside the house crying merciful to God including our daughter Mellady. She held me so tight and while she was yet crying she managed to encourage me and kept saying, "dad', it's going to be okay. I could hear her voice but at the same time my mind was in and out and the last time, it went out, I was with you but not with you. I saw the truck, I watched as your uncle drove into the woods and I saw the Gun he took out of the glove department and I watched him capture the little girl who I first laid eyes on. I watched her being forced inside of the box as the future woman you was to become ran as fast as she could but left behind the little girl no one would ever see again. I could not stop the tears nor could I not stop screaming. I tried everything I could but I was too far away. I watched the woman who looked like a child go home and live with emptiness because everything she had, was boxed in with the little girl. I watched the pain take over and torture you day and night. I watched as she let the little girl ambition, confidence, love, hopes and dreams disappear. The girl I knew who was full of life and love had given birth to a woman that looked identical to her but was far from her. I saw how every time I came around you would feel like that little girl again I just never knew she was never there, but somehow you trusted her because you gave her key to my heart. She was the little girl's pain walking on earth; she was the little girl's fears breathing in polluted air. I watched this woman fight not because she wanted to but because she did not know anyone around her, she was lost. I watched her turn to drugs and alcohol not because it was something she was into but it filled the void and the emptiness inside her and helped her cope with being in a place that she was forced into before her time. I still remember your dream and your number one goal to be a wife and the best mother ever and I watched our children appear before our eyes. I remember I asked you to marry me and you said yes but I would have to get my mom to sign for me. To think if my mom would have went alone with it we would have had even more kids and a bigger family and built so much more and probably half the stuff we went through we have never gone through. I guess it just was not the right time but I kept my promise. I told you I would marry you and take you away from all of your worries and we would be a family one day. Honestly, I did not know when and how but I knew I would. I had never loved anyone the way that I love you. You were my first love in every way and you taught me so much even how to activate the gift of a father, something that was already inside of me. You never knew, but you were never empty. In fact the little girl was smarter then you and I both. Somehow, she did not allow everything to be forced inside of the box with her, but she allowed the woman to run off with everything that she had already prepared for her. She told you all about me because she knew that I would never stop fighting for her just like she never stop fighting for that little boy who would eventually be trapped inside of a similar box.

CHAPTER 7

The Alarm Clock

The day before the accident, I remember my wife and I stayed up all night talking about everything while she was doing my hair. She was so sleepy but she did not want to stop until she was done. She said she wanted me to feel good and look good because the next day was all about me and she wanted me to be happy about the outcome. (Smile) I could see she was excited herself but nervous as well. It was going to be the first time she had ever sung in front of people besides her family. I just knew that the concert was going to be perfect especially because the rehearsals we had were great not to mention we had Anton Milton performing. I already knew that it was going to be the best concert ever. Most of all I could not wait to see and hold my first CD in my hand. It felt as though my dream was coming true and I had worked so hard and long to complete it and now the world was going to hear me. I was so happy and grateful for my wife giving me the money to make it all happen and although the concert was almost canceled because I couldn't sale all the tickets, my mom who believed in me so much and knew how much it meant to me made sure the concert was still on. Over coming so many obstacles made me believe it was a day ordained by God, it pushed me to want it even more and I was ready. After my wife was done with my hair we finally went to bed as she held the baby in her arms I held her in mine. The next day I got up an hour earlier than usual. I looked at my wife and the baby as they were sound asleep and looking as perfect as they could have possibly looked. Before leaving the house, I remember walking into the kid's room. I opened my daughter's room and as expected, she was asleep. As I opened the door to my sons room, it seemed as though he felt my presence, while yet still asleep he lifted up his head and said "I love you Dad" I responded by kissing his forehead and saying "I love you too" and he laid his head back down and went back to sleep. After I took my shower and got dress, I left the house for work expecting that day to be the best day ever. All that day in the office, I talked about the concert. I had put up a flyer on the bulletin board early that week so everyone would know. I was even sharing it with some of the guest in the hotel. Everyone seemed so excited about it as well.

Later on that day, I remember sitting in my office and then all of a sudden I looked out of my window and I could see this beautiful colorful bird flying back and forth trying to get into my truck through the passenger window. It seemed so weird that I had to grab one of my employees and asked her to look. She was as shocked as I was. The bird tried to enter the window at least three times. I did not think too much into it but it was the weirdest thing ever. I was leaving for the day and got inside my truck. Just as I was calling my wife to confirm if everyone was ready, the same bird ran into the same window again. This time it sat on the rear mirror and attempted to get inside three times, yet hitting its head each time. I called my grandmother right away. My grandmother answered the phone and I told her what had happened. I knew that birds had represented death which is why I was so scared that one was determined to get inside of my truck but my grandmother also made me aware again that it wasn't a good sign. She told me be careful and be in prayer and she did not have to say it twice because after I hung up the phone with her I immediately started praying. Finally, after pulling it together, I resumed back to being excited about my concert. My phone started vibrating and ringing. On the screen it said wifey so immediately I answered saying "what's up bae," "hey hunny, are you off yet because I don't want you to be late" she replied. "Yes bae I'm actually on my way home now, are the kids ready, I have to stop and get some shoes from the store and get a shirt to wear" I said in a very low tone. I knew she was going to go off because she always thought that I waited to the last minute to get things done but surprisingly she didn't and responded by saying "ok sweetie, just hurry home, the kids and I are both ready. "I am going to where the heels you bought me for mother's day because I know you like them a lot and I want you to be happy in every way on this day. By the way, I don't have any accessories in the color they want us to wear". "It is ok bae I replied, "we will just see if we can find something when I go to look for my stuff and I'm around the corner from the house "I said hoping that when I got there they would just be coming out. She said, "Ok I'm putting on the baby's jacket now". After hanging up the phone I pulled up to the house and parked in the front of the door. It was so weird to see three pigeons right on the doorstep. I got out the truck and realized the closer I got, that they weren't moving so I took out my phone and took a picture as close as I could but it wasn't until I reached for the door knob did they fly away. I was trying to tell my wife as soon as I walked in the house but she was handing me the baby's car seat and rushing the kids out the house. "Do you have everything you need" she asked just before shutting the door. I looked in her hands and saw that she had my suite bag and dress shoes just in case. I said yes and put the baby in the car. "How's my hair?" she asked but as I looked over to say something I noticed our two oldest kids arguing over who sits in the front seat. "I love it bae," I said as I got in the truck. She smiled and got in the truck and sat by the baby. We both closed our doors and looked at our kids still going at it over the front seat. "Enough I said, Jay you get in the front and Mellady you'll get in front on the way coming back" my wife leaned up to the front saying "bae he always sits in the front." "Your right bae I replied but she will sit in the front on the way back" I knew she wasn't satisfied so she said "the baby is sleep sweetie so I'll sit in the front" she got out and both the kids got in the backseat. We drove off and went to the grocery store. I remember her phone ringing and a woman asked her to come in for an interview at any edible arrangement store. I looked over at her and saw how happy she was. She had been out of work almost a year and a half or maybe more but she was ready to go back. She wanted to help even though I told her we were ok. When she hung up the phone the look she had on her face was of an older woman so I started laughing. "Why u laughing bae" she asked "you just looked like you were really old for a minute," but I could see it was not as funny as it was for me. "I'm sorry I said, you know you're so beautiful bae" and she smiled and looked back at the kids in the back seat as to see what they were going to say because they always did every time we would be all lovey douby in front of them. When we got to the last store we could barely find anything but there on the floor I noticed a pearl. "I know bae; you can wear a pearl necklace, bracelet, and earrings." I never saw u in pearls anyway, it would be a real elegant look," I said as I picked up the pearl from the floor. She looked at the pearl and said "ok babe". After we left the store, we headed over to the store where she had the interview. When she came out of the interview, she looked excited and happy. She got in the car and said "I think she's going to hire me bae" I looked at her and said "Why wouldn't she" she smiled and said "your rite hunny, but we got to go, u still have to pick up the cake and pick up your cousin Charlene". I definitely had forgotten about it but we got on root one and headed towards Trenton New Jersey. When we got to Sam's Club, my son got out with me and we rushed inside to get the cake for the concert. The cake was so big and looked amazing. I was even more excited and anxious. I could barely fit the cake in the truck because my sister's suite case was still inside taking up all the space but I did manage to get it in. I started making jokes about it but my wife was not having it. "Bae no joking or playing around seriously you need to be focus and concentrating on God moving, this day, we want God to have his way, and to use you even at your concert. We're going to be pure and be praying that God get the glory" I was a little upset at first because I was only joking but at the same time She was only speaking the truth and as I began to really think about it she had been acting different from the time I picked her up. It was not different in a bad way but different in sense that she was living peacefully and light that day. I thought for a quick Second that maybe she was just saying that because she was nervous because she was singing. I remember my son put in my cd the copy that my aunt had given me and he and my daughter started jamming. My wife's phone begins to ring. "It's aunt quita (my manager) bae" she said as my son turned down the radio. She wanted to know our location because it was so many people already there. She told her we were on our way to pick up my cousin and that we would be there shortly. I know my manager was not too happy about it but I had to pick up the cake she ordered. While we were exiting the business way root one heading towards Trenton my wife called my sister. It wasn't long into their conversation did all of a sudden a tractor trailer turns in front of me out of nowhere. Everything went black from there and all I heard was a loud scream that sounded like an alarm clock.

CHAPTER 8

Holding On

There were no stage, no flashing lights, no microphone, no band, and no screaming crowds. There was just space, air, and an open road in which I found myself walking on. It felt as though I had been walking on that same road all my life and was now at a point where I couldn't go any further, my strength had failed me and my feet refused to carry the weight any longer. I was choking and out of breath and with each moment I was getting weaker. There were no signs on this road, not even a yellow or white line accommodated its black face. I looked around and saw nothing but emptiness. I felt defeat wrap its arms around me and as it laid me down to sleep there was a voice in the distance that came running towards me. I felt the voice grab my hand and the tighter the grip got the more clear the voice became. The voice was speaking saying, "sir, sir, are you ok? I need you to stay with me, sir." It was a voice I had never heard before yet the words itself had latched on to me and pulled me off the road. I started to feel a warm stimulation on the tip of my fingers and suddenly a sound rushed into my head like the air that came rushing into my body. "Sir, sir are you hurt"? I heard the voice asking but did not know why until I tried to move. At that final moment, I saw the accident appear with my eyes close and all I could do was scream. "My family, my family, someone help my family" please, please, my wife and kids!" I kept repeating repeatedly. I heard the voice say, "its ok we got your family out, I just need you to stay calm, and it's going to be ok." I could feel the tears burning my eyes as I felt them rushing through the cracks of my eyelids but I refused to open them. I remember trying to move again and realized my head felt like it was about to explode. Something was squeezing my head to the point that the pain was penetrating all through my body. The voice never let my hand go. "Stay with me ok, I'm right here and where going to get you out of here ok?" I heard the voice say as I kept screaming, "why,

why, why would that truck turn in front of me"? The voice replied by saying "I know, I know, but let's focus on getting you out of here" but I could not focused at all I tried not to scream because I could not bear the pain anymore. I was getting so tired and all I wanted to do was go to sleep. As I loosened my grip, I felt the voice shack my hand. "Hey we almost got you out of here I just need you to stay awake, are you ok?" "Sir, sir, sir" the voice kept saying. "Are you ok? It asked once more as it shook my hand. "I'm ok just tired" I responded and the minute I let go of the voices hand I felt pressure lift off my head and the cold air smack me in the face. I felt arms cuff underneath my arms and pull me out of the truck. I remember lying on a bed that was moving fast. They tore off my clothes and attached so many things to my body. The last thing I heard was the sound of an emergency truck. It is not much that I remember but sometimes I felt like it should have been me or maybe HE should have taken us all but, for whatever reason He did not. I did not know and could not even imagine why. I remember crying and praying that God would perform a miraculous miracle and bring my wife and two sons back to life forgetting that he had already performed a miracle but I kept praying anyway. Sometimes I would tell myself, I had I not been sedated all that time, I could have prayed for them. I could have called on God and pleaded on their behalf. Now all I could think about was the life my family and I shared together. My mind went all the way back to the month before my wife and I got married. I remember the conversation we had over the phone that led to me asking her to marry me. It was actually the third time I had proposed to her, once was in the third grade in again when I was sixteen but this time she said yes. See I was the one who wanted to plan this big wedding and be all-fancy but she just wanted to get married. I kept trying to convince her that I wanted to see her walk to me in a beautiful big dress. She thought the idea was nice but she just wanted to have my last name. "I'm not caught up on all of that" I remember her saying but I told her it was a dream of mine and I wanted to sing to her. Finally, she agreed as long as I did not spend too much money. I remember that day as if it was yesterday. I could hear her screaming "I'm getting married everybody!" "You're not going to marry no body mella" her family responded in the background. The kids had to have been right next to her because I heard her say "yes I am, and then very quietly, mommies going to marry daddy and we're going to live as a family again." I could hear them laughing in the background. She was so happy and excited but not as excited as I was. I had loved her since the third grade and never stopped. I was finally going to fulfill the promise I had made to her so long ago. I remember we stayed on the phone for hours and talked about all the arrangements. One day when I came home from work, we went to sleep on the phone going back and forth, about where we were going to live. We went on and on about rather or not I was moving down south again or rather or she was going to move to the city. I remember she didn't want to leave the four bedroom brick house she was about to move in but when I told her that I would take care of her and our kids as a man should she was convinced and trusted me to do just what I had said, so she made the decision to leave it all behind. Weeks later we both could not take being away from each other any longer and decided to get married as soon as we could. Before I knew it, she had quit both her jobs and I was on my way back down south to get my family. I did not have time to get any flowers or any jewelry I just left, and did not think twice about it but none of it mattered because I gave her me and she felt like the queen of the world. I admire that fact it did not take much to make her happy, I could give her a flower from a tree and she would smile all day. Man, I loved her with every organ in my body. Although she was scared out of her mind to leave her family behind and move to the big city, she was determined to live in love. I remember I had tried my best to plan everything. I knew she didn't' want anything too big but I wanted to make it at least nice enough that she would be happy. Everything was going so well until we had to choose who was going to marry us. It had become a bigger issue then we had expected. The communication between our families had gotten so bad that we had decided not to have a wedding or reception at all. She kept repeating, "The devil is not going to still our joy". I remember just laughing and agreeing to whatever it was that she wanted to do. I had been working for Wal-Mart for about three and half years and at that time I was their Pharmacy department Manager when I had received a phone call from her asking "are you sure you want to marry me love"? I responded by saying, "yes of course". She then asked me "If you could marry me right now would you do it". I remember telling her "I will drop everything and do it right now". She said "good, did you take your lunch break" I said "no but why bae, what's going on" that's when she said, "I found a judge that will marry us right now so you have to take your lunch and leave now." I was so shocked and surprised that she had even made those arrangements. I looked at the phone and smiled. I said to her "that's impossible bae because it would take at least twenty minutes to get to my job and about twenty minutes to get to the court house." Then she replied "oh I know sweetie, that's why you need to go clock out now for lunch and come out side because were here already" I had to catch my breath but as soon as she said she was there I rushed to the back and clocked out. I left work immediately and we got married on my lunch break. I will never forget that day. That day I vowed to spend the rest of my life with my wife. The memory is what I hold on to because it is a memory that would always remind me of how strong and true our love really was. Life was pushing against me and at the time, I did not know it at all. I cannot say what it took me to hold on, but I know I held on. I held on with the grip of my fingertips. As I look back and think about it, even now chills run all over my body. It does scare me at times because I think about the fact that I should not be here, I should not have made it out of something so tragic. Maybe it's just me but sometimes air seems so hard to come by and happiness seems so expensive, besides who's to say if you buy it you'll always have it, best advice is to hold on to it while it's still yet visible in your hands.

CHAPTER 9

A Soldier

I was hurting and never said a word but He held my heart I was walking with no direction and somehow you became my map I couldn't speak but you heard every word and at my lowest point you reminded me of who I was. All this time you never changed and to think I was searching elsewhere, your love just never disappeared no matter how far I pushed you away. So now, you know I am never letting go because I cannot make it without you. Oh yea, thank you.

Lonely, I am. I can hear you asking me now, where are all those people? Where are all people who surrounded you in the beginning? Where is the ones who promised and who gave their word, where are the ones whose assignment was to stick by your side especially through everything that you are going through, where are they? I know what you are asking. I asked the same question as I saw them slowly disappear. It just feel like I don't' matter anymore. Do you remember how you used to make me feel, as if I was important or more so like it was all about me? Well now I'm chasing after attention but you know how I am with my pride so I don't say that I need it, I try to show that I do but no one seems to know my mind like you do. Everyone gets everything wrong about me. Baby these people are envying me for no reason. Their looking at me as if they hate me. I do not understand what I did wrong. I did not ask for this life, I did not ask for a story like this. How did I become so strong, baby how am I able to wake up in the morning and say God I still love you, look in the mirror and say you are okay, or smile with my head lifted? They do not even know that I want to break down and never stop crying. They do not know that I need love and not just the love that last for a couple of days or comes and goes but the love that is strong enough to occupy the spaces that filled my heart. I gave so much and ended up empty only hoping that they would stay but just like anyone would, they took everything that

I was giving and when they did not see any more coming or that it was no longer coming fast enough, they took off. I had allowed them not to just take off but to take off with a piece of me. I tell you what though baby you were right and I just thought that you just said it because of the way I acted but I found out that I love God more then I loved life. When I thought that, I would walk away and not ever feel that I could love him as I did, I realized I had fallen in love with him even more. Baby to some people it is so hard to believe but I know for certain that God loves me not just because he kept me here but because He has come through so many times afterwards and he has never stopped providing for me and our daughter. Speaking of our daughter, baby she is every bit of you. I still cannot believe that you did so much without me even knowing but then again you were always ahead of the game. Our daughter wants to be a doctor and a singer like me. Her favorite color is still pink but now it is purple just like yours. She is getting tall. Can you believe it? She is getting ready to go to the six grade. Baby already the boys are in her face but of course I be praying because you know I do not think too well with that situation. She has your strength though and she has a strong mind just as we had hoped she would. She talks about you and the boys a lot and not in a way that she is angry but in a way that she knows you guys where not just a fairy tale and that your still there in her heart. We do a lot of talking and doing things together. I did exactly what I said I would and brought her this necklace and promise ring and one day after dinner at a restaurant in front of everyone I got down on one knee and asked her to accept my promise to love her and be there for her and protect her and she said yes. Some people looked at us as if we were strange but others heard me and thought, it was just the cutest and sweetest thing any dad could have ever done. I must say baby she keeps me going. If it was not for her being the way she is, I do not know what I would do. We pray together and read our bible together a lot. This I have to tell you because it was incredible and a night that I know you would forever remember. We were having a conversation the night before about her calling and her purpose in life and the next night we went to church the man of God said the same exact things we were discussing. He confirmed that she was a prophetess and she was going to be preaching all over the world and it was exactly what she had told me the night before. She also had said that night before that she wanted to receive the gift of tongues because she was filled with the Holy Ghost. I admit I was somewhat surprised that she knew the difference but after the man of God spoke, we were just about to leave and I could not have left out of the church without giving confirmation to what exactly he had said so without hesitation I did. Before I knew it, the man of God said to her that if she wanted to receive the gift of tongues that she did not have to wait but that she could get it at that moment. She spoke out immediately that she wanted it. The man of God immediately called her to the alter and asked if I would accompany her as I did. After maybe an hour she was crying and laid out on the alter with sweat and tears dripping down her face and saliva hanging from her mouth onto the floor. Just as the fresh wind entered into the sanctuary and into her body, it took rest in her belly and so it came rushing out in the form of an unknown language. She left that night with a new look and a new demeanor about herself. It was as if she grew up overnight. In spite of what she had been through and faced in life, she had become that Soldier you had always wanted to be. I know you see but I just wanted to let you know that we are stronger then we have ever been.

CHAPTER 10

Missing Out

"Daddy when I grow up, I want to be just like you". My son looked at me and with those words that came out his mouth; I could die repeatedly just knowing that I will never see him be anything. I remember him smiling when he spoke those words and at that moment, it was everything I would always want to hold on to. He had come such a long way. I remember as he was growing up not being able to speak correctly, his self-esteem was as low as the ground, but over the years he became so smart, respectful, well spoken, and his confidence was as high as his head (smiling). Everywhere I went he went with me imitating my steps, my words, and my ways of thinking. I wish I could wipe away his tears, all of his fears, and bad dreams. I wanted to be that dad he could always depend on, his protector, his confident, the one who he would talk about his girlfriend to, talk about college, work, losing his virginity, or who he would fall in love with, and who he would marry. I wanted to be there for the times he would go through, the times he would be hurt, and the times he would need someone there. My son is gone and I will never see him again. I didn't say goodbye, I didn't get to crack a joke like we usually do, nor did I get the chance to hold his hand, kiss his forehead, pick him up on my shoulders, or most importantly tell him that I love him with everything in me. I often think about the times him and I would get away from the girls and just chill. Our father and son time was always funny and exciting. Everywhere we went everyone just seemed to notice us. People always thought I was his brother and if I be honest we did act that way sometimes. Man I loved to see him laugh. He was such a clown just like me and once you got us started, it was hard to get us to stop. Sometimes they could not stand us though because we were just alike in so many ways but we brought life to a dull day. He was just starting to mature so much more especially in his singing and ways of thinking.

I was starting to see the God in him that, most adults did not have. He respected and loved me so much, that I knew. He thought I was his world, his superhero and I was. I was everything he wanted me to be because I loved him that much. I just wish I could tell him repeatedly how much I really loved him and was grateful to have had such an intelligent, brilliant, and handsome son like him. Although I may never get a chance to see him grow up, graduate, go through life's obstacles, or become the best man he would have been, still, I enjoyed his short life that God had allowed me to be a part of.

"I'll never leave your side, no matter what I say nor do, I love you." My wife would always say after every intense argument and those words pull at my heart every single day. She was supposed to be my forever and I hers. We were supposed to see who got gray hairs first or who started to feel old and look it first. Either way we were supposed to live and die together in an unbreakable love. I have seen the smile on her face that lite up my world and made me feel like the king that I wanted to be. She was the motivation behind my drive and the ropes that kept me from falling out of the ring. Who would have thought, I would never have another moment to look into her eyes, breath the same air as she did, hold and caress her body, and shield her from hurt and pain? We were supposed to have a big wedding for our five-year mark of marriage and more kids before we were 35. We were supposed to teach all of our kids how to be a good man and woman, how to cook, clean, to be a good provider for their family, how to be strong independent and serve God with all their heart and soul. We were supposed to accomplish our goals and dreams together. I will never see how she responds to the things that our kids would have one day got into. I will never get the chance for her and me to be grandparents together and spoil our grandchildren. I will never taste another meal more less look at her in another beautiful dress or stylish pair of shoes. I will never spend another holiday or birthday with her. I would miss everything we had ever dreamed of together. She spoiled me in every way and I felt paralyzed without her. Sometimes I sit back and watch my daughter smile and laugh and all I can think about Is my wife missing every moment but even more so how my daughter would miss out on having her mother in her life. It brings tears to my eyes and sadness in my heart majority of the times when other families are around her or other kids is with their moms because I can only imagine how she must feel. She is only a child and even though she is so strong and very intelligent for her age, she still understands pain. I often try to find ways just to keep her smiling or her mind off what we been through but she has already learned how to embrace the path that she been given. Of course, we have our days and our moments even sometimes together but God is so awesome that he sends a wind of peace even at that moment. My wife would be very proud of her. There are so many days and nights were I often just reminisce. Unbelievably, sometime that keeps me going. Our life was never perfect but a life I enjoyed. I could say all the problems or issues we may have had but when I think about it, those issues where never as big as we thought they were and the problems and issues made us love each other as much as we did. I will miss everything thing about her, but I will always treasure and cherish our life together forever in my heart. I know In spite of how crazy it may sound but at this point I'm ok now to know that the last gift that she desired most, was another child and she was able to carry him home with her in heaven.

CHAPTER 11

Words of Inspiration

To some people crying is a sign of weakness but for me my tears represent strength. Although my heart may have its own struggle, I refuse to abort the mission. I know that life will hit u with everything it possibly can even with the things you have voluntarily given it; however, I have been in God's plan from the very beginning and I can see progress.

"Never settle for less when your life is worth so much more, everything behind you should not be keeping you but pushing you forward for destiny lies ahead."

"When your purposed to shine, you never let anyone or anything dim your light"

#lettherebelight

"When you want more, you go after more and you let nothing stop you."
#settlingisnotanoption

"Darkness is the image that covers what is perceived to be unknown but the unknown is never not known when you have the ability to see through the dark; therefore, see your destiny"
#notsubjectednoraffected
#movingforward

"Why listen with your ears when you can hear with your heart, What's real, you will feel."
#humanabilities

"If you must trust, trust only the substance within the glass and never the crack, in the glass."
#tearstrappedintheglass

"What you are experiencing now is just preparation for your promise on tomorrow. It's gonna happen, you just have to see it."

"Love has its own strength, and if it's strong enough, it will fight for you."
#stronglove
#unbreakable

"An upgrade is something better, something better has more value, more value is more appreciated, by the right person."
#feelingappreciated

"A conqueror knoweth not how the fight begins, but knoweth victory, shall be the end."
#wisdomNexperience

"If you said no with your lips but yes with your actions, you had no discipline & true faithfulness"
#menNwomenofstandards
#strongwill

"Sometimes you have to experience heart trauma to remind you, who you are and how strong you are."
#lifelessons

"Real determination has no retirement plan, just endless capabilities, to reach it's endless goals and dreams."
#livingdetermined

"Nothing can stand in the way of your dream, except your will to believe."
#wingsR4flying

"If your success doesn't come to you, who's to say u can't go to it? It is your will to conquer that which has not yet been conquered."
#missioninprogress

"LOVE should never have a limit but if it does, there should never be a penalty for going beyond it."
#Lovegoesthedistance

"It's not about the struggles you go through, just the struggles that make you."
#yougotthis

"Make change, not just a name"
#positiveimpact

"When your worth more, you require more, and if you require more, it's because you know more, and when you know more, dont accept lack, any more."
#whenyourworthisvalued
#moretaughtme2neverlack

"Never focus on the uncertain, the momentarily, or the occasional, but focus on the consistant, the final, and the assured. Someday it will be more than just a dream."
#Lifewisdom

"Be that train that's moving, and everyday, pick up speed."
#goaftermore

"How can it be over I'f our still living; therefore, what is incomplete is just the beginning of what you see it to be."
#Aviewofgrateness

"The harder the struggle, the bigger the muscle"
#flexinainteasy

"What really matters, is what you go after most."
#dreamsNsucess

"An excuse is a way to escape and avoid truth, but an apology is a way to change and do better."
#ifyouonlyknewbetteryouwoulddobetter

"When you've gone so far, and yet it seems not far enough, cross the line."
#pushed

"Dreams don't give up, we do."
#determinationgetsresults

"You can choose to ignore truth, but you can never erase it."
#neverbeinjudicious

"When the wrong people walk out of your life, the right people walk in."
#venerated

"Things change with time, & we only got time, to live."
#decipherwhoyouR

"Failure to listen, results in everything missing"
#nomoreinclination

"Deny less & accept more"
#beexceptional

CHAPTER 12

Life

Here it is not even two years later and I feel like I am literally in the wilderness but I am not worried. I know that God is going to work it out; however, yes, it hurts so bad and feels so cold did I forget to add lonely? I do so much for others and there seems to be no one on my side. In fact, I can be around hundreds of people and still feel abandon. Its situations like this that makes me confused about my purpose but I know that it is a setup. I look out the gigantic window that is next to me and I stare right into the sky and lose myself in the gray yet slight blue clouds. I forget my problems and try to see the dream that I have had since I was a little boy. A part of me says this is the real world and in this world there is no such thing as magic but the other part of me says that of course there is no magic but dreams can and will come true if only you believe. Sometimes I feel like that is my problem, I believe too much. Sometimes I do feel like I'm holding on for nothing and nothing will ever become of my life and I just wasted so much time; however, with the way I was created, even with all of those thoughts in my head, I still couldn't let go, not even if I wanted to. There is something inside of me, which is much stronger than I am. Something inside of me that has a strength that I can never began to describe. It will not let me go nor will it allow me to let go. I am holding on and having faith not because I want to but the something inside me controls my will. Can you imagine being in a world alone and not knowing what to do or where to go? I have no idea where to start. I wonder if there was a specific place to start life all over again. There has to be some type of guidelines. Am I really just supposed to figure this thing out on my own? It really seems to be that way especially because I know people and I have a big family yet I am here. I just feel as though I do not matter. How could I possibly matter when no one is concerned about my life or where I am now? It is cold out here, but now that I think about it, I am always so cold until now it is starting to be comforting. I really feel like the world has abandoned me. (Abandoned, yea that word definitely seems to be the closest to what I am trying to say). I see so many colors everywhere; however, where is my color? I can hear the conversations of other people around me. Where is the conversation of my own? Where is someone who will sit down with me and have a conversation? Who cares to know my name, Will anyone ask me why I am here, or more so what is it that I am writing? Does anyone see that I am here? Am I not noticeable? I am tired of making mistakes in my life and not knowing what has to come of it. I did not plan for my life to be this way I didn't plan for this story to be the reason for my tears. I did not 'ask to have a story at all. I guess this would be a better story told as a fairy tale. It is funny, just a little anyway, maybe. People would like to read about things that seem to be so far fetching, drawn out, negative and dramatic, I get it, but what about the real stories. Stories that are being unfold every day and not just any story, but the stories that cry out for help. No one really bothers to listen or even read them. These stories are the ones that are unheard or not talked about. It is a cruel world and so many people make this world seem as if living in it is a tormenting prison cell. Someone one please get rid of this lobby music. Oh yeah, where am I? I was actually wondering when you would ask that question. I am sitting inside of a fast food restaurant. I know you are wondering why and I was going to tell you earlier but I was a little afraid; however, I am not now. I am here because I have no electricity in my home. Yeah, me, the person who you thought had this glamorous life. I am so sorry to disappoint you. I am a real person with real problems but at the end of the day, I also serve a real God. Since the altering of my life, I have learned that God test us all the time especially our faith. He wants to know how much we truly love him. Is not our love only felt and shown when HE is good to us or spoils us with our wants and desires? What about when HE takes our happiness for a while or removes the sun and gives us darkness instead or better yet when HE holds the rain and everything around us including our life is dry and seems so pointless. Where is the love then? People are not aware of the life beyond the pain and suffering. Some people need to know that they are never alone. I know for me that was something I so desperately needed to know. It is so important for someone to be there and not just say they will. People will never know how important or just how powerful it is for someone to know there is a consistent love. To be honest I thought my life was over when my family left this world but now that I see things more clearly, I realize that it is actually the start of my life. I have heard the voice before but it's not until now that I have chosen to listen. I choose to follow the path that God has set for me. The most important thing that I have learned thus far, is that life is not just the breath in the body that causes you to be alive but life is purpose and coincides with destiny because without purpose or destiny your existence is meaningless. You have life and are alive by default but you are living and striving to reach destiny when you know your purpose.

CHAPTER 13

The Last Heart beat

Two thousand and thirteen was the most important year to me because it is in fact the last time I heard my own heartbeat. Sometimes I wondered if I was preparing for what was to come and because it could have been a possibility, there were other times I hated myself. Why was not there a way for me to change what was already going to be.

My family and I were very close and we never told too many people our business because we knew the results of that; however, at this time Facebook was more so like a journal for my wife and me. Although she rarely used it except to keep in contact with her family, I on the other hand did. It was not until now that I realized everything that I had written, was already purposed.

As I begin to review my timeline, the tears begin to flow down my cheeks, in the same column, as they had seemed to always flow.

February seventh two thousand and thirteen: Preparing myself for the Voice Auditioning this Saturday. God, whatever door you open I am walking in it. (Greater is coming)

February eighth two thousand and thirteen: Performing at the Wal-Mart in Bristol PA for black history Month on February twenty third at three pm. Hope to see everyone there!

February twelfth two thousand thirteen: Preparing for Sunday's Best Audition. This is it he said in his word that your gift would make room enough for me. Fans and Family please keep praying.

February fourteenth two thousand thirteen: Happy V day to my beautiful wife, my two little ones, and one on the way. They are my hearts and the best valentine's gift. To my fans and family sending you all my love Happy V Day.

February sixteenth two thousand thirteen: Here at Sunday best I'm going up in a little I hope everyone's praying.

I didn't make it but that don't mean it's the end I know one thing I got my camera time in lol It don't mean stop we just getting started. Look out for my CD Never Alone coming soon.

February twenty fourth two thousand and thirteen: To God be the glory thank you to all my fans, friends, and family who came out to support me it means a lot love you much.

March first two thousand and thirteen: When you have too much to lose, giving up is not an option.

March nineteenth two thousand and thirteen: My wife b day is almost over it was wonderful just to see her smile just because it's a great feeling. I love you sweetie. Happy B Day.

March twenty third two thousand and thirteen: My baby is here! To my wife I love you sweetie you are an amazing woman.

March twenty fourth two thousand and thirteen: So happy that God bless me with another boy on March twenty third two thousand and thirteen. Five pounds, fifteen ounces, and nineteen inches. I'm so grateful I have the greatest wife ever three down how many more bae lol.

March thirtieth two thousand and thirteen: In spite of

what I'm going through I'm holding on for I am in faith mode at this moment. I don't know what Gods going to do but I need him to do it.

April eighth two thousand and thirteen: I came home to this birthday cake. Its lunch time again lol I guess I'll be doing pushups and sit ups all night.

April seventeenth two thousand and thirteen: Its hard to keep your head up when all the evidence around you shows its over so expect for faith to hurt but its worth the strength gained.

April twenty-seventh two thousand and thirteen: Lord touch my life and command everything to line up especially my finances. Thanking you in advance.

March twelfth two thousand and thirteen: Happy mother's day mom I love you.

March twenty second two thousand and thirteen: Bible study was awesome tonight. Talking about the fruits of the spirit definitely makes you exam yourself.

July tenth two thousand and thirteen: Ok, I need major support!!! I have about fifty tickets left to sell before the end of the next week. Please support if not a donation is much appreciated. Contact me or my manager Larquista

Stephens as soon as possible. You don't want to miss this amazing event.

July seventh two thousand and thirteen: I hear a song in my spirt "You don't know my story" Lord Jesus every day is getting harder than the day before. Too bad I'm at work because I feel like purging. I claim victory right now in the name of Jesus. I pray the rest of your day and mine goes well.

July twentieth two thousand and thirteen: I have never been so stressed in all my days I am beyond sick of people and their lip service you not getting paid for why do it. All I can say is I will not be down forever, for the bible says "be not weary in well doing for you shall reap if you faint not".

July twenty second two thousand and thirteen: I feel like pressing on, though trials come on every side I feel like pressing on. I woke up this morning and its taking everything in me to get up because I'm in this storm and I can't see but I hear the song I feel like pressing on. As I encourage myself I encourage you, get a pressing in your spirit. Don't let the cares of this world stop you from moving forward. The devil may have block some things in your life but I hear the Lord saying "but when you have suffered enough in this season then shall you see my glory and you shall see again how great thou are".

July twenty eighth two thousand and thirteen was our four-year anniversary and four days later was August second, two thousand and thirteen. That was the day of my cd release party. We just knew it was going to be an amazing and exciting day for us all; however, what we did not know it would in fact be the day that would separate us all, forever.

Can you see the very thing that I did not see? It was a warning, a warning that told me something was about to happen and that whatever it was I would surely have to have more in me then I have ever had before. Looking back, after everything forced out of me, I cannot seem to understand how that would have been possible. Just like an empty bottle, there was nothing inside me. Although it seemed as if my heart were left abandoned on an open highway, I realize that God had to do what I did not expect, ask for, or was even prepared for, in order to give me the experience to assure me exactly who HE was, and that, I found out in the midst of the hurricane. After the angry and vicious rain stood still and the heavy wind ceased,

I knew that life should not have occupied this vessel but because HE is El-Shaddai, God all mighty I was breathing and living as I always have been. I have a heart now that can worship him in spirit and in truth and a testimony that tells the world that man is exactly what he is, a man and that the Lord thou God, He is... and if your reading this, you know the rest.

To the Man that caused the tragic accident,

I don't know you. I don't know anything about you nor have I ever seen your face, but I want you to know that I forgive you. I forgive you and I love you with the Love of God. Yes, I could hate you, I could want to hurt you, or even want you to feel what I feel if, I spoke or respond according to the pain that I feel in my heart but needless to say I do believe or give you the benefit of the doubt without even knowing you, that you didn't wake up that morning and say "I'm going to kill a family today"; however, with your carelessness you did.

I wanted so bad to hurt you even with my words because I felt as if there was nothing else I could do, and had no other way to pay you back for your carelessness but I'm not a violent or mean person and I truly know that at the end of the day it still wouldn't make me feel any better.

Although I do forgive you, I have yet to understand why you haven't asked for forgiveness. I have yet to understand why I don't know you or maybe know your family. I understand that we are human and in being a human we are going to forever make mistakes but should we not acknowledge and correct our mistakes? If we can't correct our mistakes, should we not try our hardest to show how apologetic we are for making those mistakes? At least I would, especially if I was in your shoes. Yes, after being angry for so long, I did think about you. I often thought about how you must feel and if you had a wife and kids, how they must feel as well, but regardless of what I thought, I can only think now that it doesn't matter because no one, not even you, have yet to make some type of contact to say how deeply apologetic you are. No one has even attempt to see how me and my now ten year old daughter is doing or coping with the lost of three members of our family and not just any three but a wife, mother , son and brother. Although I don't understand, it is not my place to hold you or your family to what was or wasn't done, only God.

It has not been easy and certainly not something my daughter and I will ever forget. There have been good days and Lord knows some bad, but with God we are striving every day to live. You may never understand the physical and mental pain that we endure every day that the Lord allows us to see but I want you to know that we pray for you. We don't pray for harm or death upon you but we prayyou're your strength and most importantly mercy and grace.

Our family is never coming back and we have to pick up the pieces and try to make the best of what we have been given to make the best of. I'm still trying to figure out what I'm doing but I know that God is with us and he has spared us for a reason. I want you to understand that there is no amount of time you can spend in prison that will bring my family back or even erase what you have done; therefore your prison time no longer matters to me but your soul is something that matters and is very much important to God. Even in this I know that God will get the glory somehow, I just pray that one of the ways is you becoming a better person that you've ever been before. That you are cautious with any and everything that you do and that you love God with your life and being an example of God's love to other men, including the world, so that you too might win souls to bring him glory. At least that would make my families death not in vein.

Sincerely,

Shaqwan Tisdale

My Daughter

In Loving memory of Jamella, Javeon, & Musik Tisdale

Printed in the United States
By Bookmasters